Listen, Honey...

Words of Wine and Wisdom from Emerson Quillin

RUNNING PRESS
PHILADELPHIA · LONDON

Library of Congress Control Number: 2008935018

ISBN 978-0-7624-3489-3

Running Press Book Publishers
2300 Chestnut Street
Philadelphia, PA 19103-4371

Visit us on the web!
www.runningpress.com

Introduction

As we get older, we gather a lot of wisdom. Over time we mix in some wit with our wisdom and share that concoction with friends and others over drinks. Life lessons reveal themselves like never before. Whether whining over wine, meeting over margaritas, or cajoling over coffee, we connect with our companions. Quip after quip, this little book will keep you company, like girlfriends who comfort you with "Listen, honey . . ."

Let's drink to that!

Cheers!

TEENAGERS

TIRED OF BEING HASSLED
  BY YOUR STUPID PARENTS.

MOVE OUT. GET A JOB,
  PAY YOUR OWN BILLS...
  WHILE YOU STILL KNOW
      EVERYTHING!

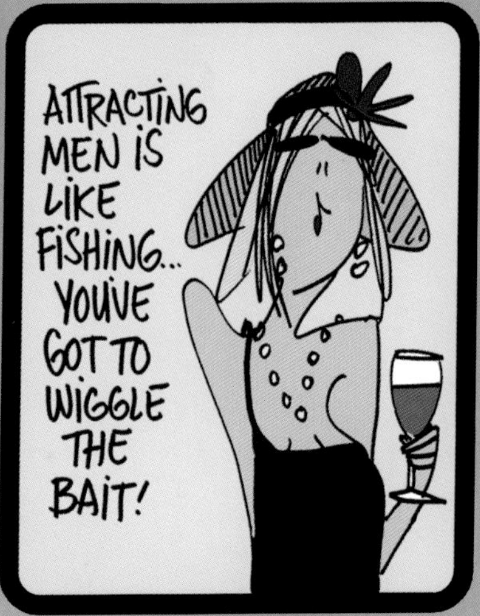
ATTRACTING MEN IS LIKE FISHING... YOU'VE GOT TO WIGGLE THE BAIT!

IF YOU'RE THINKING,
WHAT I'M THINKING, THEN
YOU'RE SICKER THAN I
THOUGHT!

WINE MAKES YOU FEEL
THE WAY YOU OUGHT TO
FEEL WITHOUT WINE.

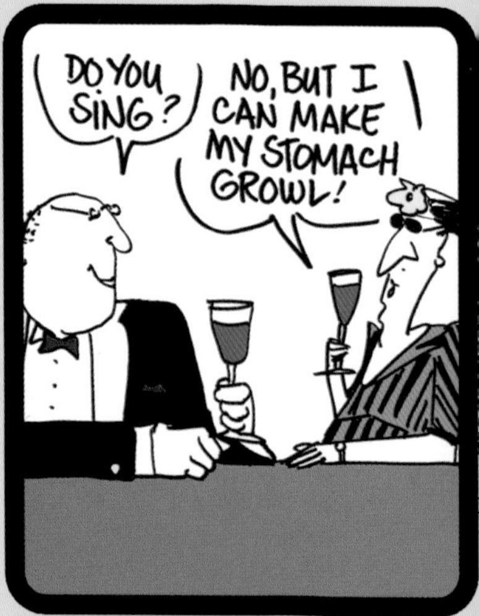
DO YOU SING?
NO, BUT I CAN MAKE MY STOMACH GROWL!

My blood type is coffee.

WINE DRIPPERS

I WANT TO THANK ALL THE
PEOPLE WHO HELPED
ME GET HERE...
MY FATHER, MY MOTHER,
AND HER OBSTETICIAN

About the Artist

Emerson Quillin grew up in Bloomfield, Indiana and received his Master Degree in textile design from Rhode Island School of Design. He moved on to become Creative Director for Champion Products of Rochester, NY, and Creative Director for Velva Sheen Sportswear of Cincinnati, Ohio, where he developed the now famous Quillin Script. His illustrations have been licensed by Emerson Street (Rochester, NY) for T-shirts, mugs, calendars, greeting cards, etc., and his work is exhibited in both private and public collections. He currently resides in Lexington, KY, and you can also find him at www.emersonshumor.com.

This book has been bound using
handcraft methods and Smyth-sewn
to ensure durability.

Designed by
Josh McDonnell.

Written and illustrated by
Emerson Quillin.

Arranged by
T.L. Bonaddio.

The text was set in
Blockhead.